POKÉMON
HOW TO TRAIN YOUR POKÉMON

Written by Lawrence Neves

WITHDRAWN

CONTENTS

INTRODUCTION

You want to catch your first Pokémon! What's next? This book will introduce you to the incredible world of Pokémon—you'll learn all the basics about what Pokémon are, where to find them, and how to train and feed your Pokémon. Get ready to start your very own Pokémon adventure!

GETTING STARTED

WHAT IS A POKÉMON?

Pokémon are unique creatures. They all have their own special powers, abilities, and personalities! Some Pokémon live in the wild, while others coexist peacefully in the human world.

Pikachu

Pikachu's cheek pouch stores electricity

Distinctive pointed ears

Tail shaped like a lightning bolt

Trainers

The people who catch and coach Pokémon are called Trainers. They raise their Pokémon to be happy, healthy, and to compete in friendly battles!

Squirtle

Helpful Pokémon

Pokémon can use their skills to help humans with their jobs. For example, some Squirtle help fight fires with the Squirtle Firefighting Squad, and some Wigglytuff can help give medical aid in Pokémon Centers.

Come find us!

Pokémon have been found in all the currently known regions of the Pokémon world—from Kanto to Galar.

POKÉMON ORIGINS

Most Pokémon hatch from Eggs! Pokémon Eggs have identifying marks that hint at which Pokémon is inside. Waiting to find out what Pokémon your Egg will hatch into can be really exciting!

Togepi

Togepi's shell is brightly decorated

A perfect match!

When two compatible Pokémon are left at the Pokémon Day Care they will eventually produce a Pokémon Egg. An Egg is ready to hatch once it begins to glow.

Egg-cellent work!

To help the Egg you receive from the Pokémon Day Care hatch you should:

- 🔴 Treat it with loving care.
- 🔴 Polish it with a warm, soft cloth.
- 🔴 Take it with you as you travel.

Ash's Eggs

Famous Trainer Ash had a number of his Pokémon hatch from Eggs, such as Phanpy, Scraggy, and Riolu.

Phanpy

Scraggy

Riolu

TRAINERS

Trainers are characters who raise, mentor, and coach their Pokémon in friendship and battle! Skilled Trainers can become Gym Leaders. They usually challenge opponents to Pokémon battles in Gyms—big arenas or battling grounds.

Goh

Ash

Unfriendly coaches

Not everyone is cut out to be a Pokémon Trainer. Occasionally, you will find Trainers, like Paul from Veilstone City in Sinnoh, who aren't very nice people. Paul treats his Pokémon unkindly and uses them just to win battles.

Paul

Meet Ash!

The most well-known Trainer is Ash Ketchum. Ash began his Pokémon journey long ago and always works hard to train his Pokémon. Ash has a very strong relationship with his Pikachu.

Badge of honor

After defeating a Gym Leader, you receive a badge. This proves to everyone you won the Gym battle in that region.

GREAT FRIENDS

Trainers are not alone in the Pokémon world.
There are various helpers who will guide Trainers
on their journey. You might meet:

- Nurse Joy—she is an expert in healing Pokémon.
- Officer Jenny—she's the law! Jenny protects
  Pokémon and people from crime.
- Professors—there's one in every region. They know
  everything there is to know about Pokémon!

Professor Oak

Officer Jenny

Nurse Joy

Useful advice

A Professor can help a Trainer by offering lots of useful advice. They can give technical data on Pokémon through a Pokédex and inform Trainers about the dangers they may find along their journey.

Special skills

Coordinators and Connoisseurs have specialized knowledge about Pokémon. Connoisseurs, like Cilan from Unova region, have the difficult job of making sure a Pokémon and Trainer are perfectly matched. A Coordinator makes sure a Pokémon looks beautiful for contests and pageants.

Cilan

Other important helpers

Ash meets many new friends on his quest to become a Pokémon Master. They all have different skills and abilities such as:

- Brock—Pokémon Breeder and chef
- Serena—talented Pokémon Performer
- Solana—brave Pokémon Ranger

EQUIP YOURSELF

Trainers need various tools and equipment to help them out throughout their adventures. The first tool you need to catch Pokémon is a Pokédex. This tool is an electronic encyclopedia of Pokémon facts and figures. It can:

- Tell you a Pokémon's height, weight, and type.
- Help identify Pokémon habitats.
- Educate a Trainer about a Pokémon's needs.

Rotom Phone

Pokédex styles

Pokédexes change in appearance as technology improves. Professor Cerise gives Ash a smartphone that is possessed by a Rotom. This Rotom Phone has a Pokédex and a lot of new fun features!

To the max!

Dynamax is a phenomenon where a Pokémon grows to many times its normal size. Trainers can control this transformation by wearing a Dynamax Band. A few Pokémon species can even Gigantamax. These Pokémon become huge, have unique powers, and often gain a different appearance.

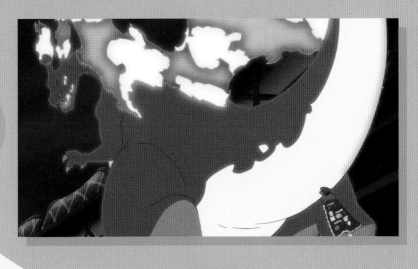

Z-Rings

Z-Rings are cool gadgets that contain Z-Crystals. They allow Trainers to access Z-Moves. These are super powerful moves that only certain Pokémon can carry out!

HAVING A BALL

Poké Balls are containers carried by Trainers to catch and carry Pokémon during their travels. They are thrown at opposing Pokémon in order to catch them. Some balls are better at catching Pokémon than others. The steps are:

- Weaken a Pokémon by battling it with another Pokémon or using a potion.
- Throw a Poké Ball at the weakened Pokémon.
- Wait for the Poké Ball to rock back and forth and turn from white back to its original color.
- If successful, you have caught the Pokémon in the Poké Ball.

Weaken them first

The weaker a Pokémon is, the better the chance is that you will catch it. However, some Pokémon are happy to be caught and don't put up a fight!

Specialty Balls

There are many types of Poké Balls, all with unique specialties. A Net Ball, for example, is great for catching Water-type and Bug-type Pokémon. A Beast Ball is perfect for capturing Ultra Beasts.

Quick Ball

Ultra Ball

Premier Ball

Timer Ball

Great Ball

Repeat Ball

Master Ball

Net Ball

TRAINER REQUIREMENTS

It takes hard work and dedication to be a Pokémon Trainer but the rewards are great. Here are some Trainer basics you need to know when getting started:

- Pick your Pokémon partner wisely—you have a choice when you get your first Pokémon of Fire-type, Grass-type, or Water-type. Choose carefully!
- Care for your Pokémon—Pokémon have lots of needs you need to be aware of.
- Know your Pokémon—you will be spending a lot of time with them, so make sure to learn as much about them as possible!

Dawn traveled with Ash in Sinnoh

Buizel

Pansage

Why train?

There are lots of reasons to become a Pokémon Trainer! Traveling the world with your Pokémon pal is great fun. However, most importantly, being a Trainer teaches you all about teamwork, confidence, and determination.

Dwebble

The journey begins

From the age of 10, Trainers can begin their journey to catch and coach Pokémon. However, it is never too late to start learning and caring about Pokémon!

TRAIN YOUR OWN WAY

There is no one way to train your Pokémon. Some Trainers focus on battles, others on friendship, and some even train their Pokémon to commit crimes!

However, all good Trainers share a bond with their Pokémon and care for them greatly.

All types of Trainers

There are many different types of Pokémon Trainers. Some like to specialize in just one type of Pokémon and become experts.

Misty
Water-type

Iris
Dragon-type

Kiawe
Fire-type

James

Jessie

Meowth

Wobbuffet

Team Rocket

If there's trouble, it is usually the work of Team Rocket! Jessie and James work for crime boss Giovanni to capture Pokémon. These mischievous Trainers often clash against Ash and his friends.

Tough love

Though Jessie and James use their Pokémon for wild schemes, they would never harm them. They show their love for their Pokémon by working closely as a team.

PICKING A POKÉMON

FINDING POKÉMON

You can find Pokémon everywhere across the known regions of the Pokémon world. Most Pokémon live in the wild. Here are some places to look:

- Trees—some Pokémon hang around on branches, so be sure to look up.
- Lakes and seas—many types of Pokémon live underwater and need to be caught on a fishing line.
- Forests and grassy fields—you might be lucky to find a Pokémon walking along a path.
- Caves—in the darkness, you might see Zubat or other cave-dwelling Pokémon.
- Big cities—some Pokémon like to hide in buildings like museums and shops.

Some Zubat live in deep, dark caves

Some Bulbasaur live in forests

Why catch at all?

A Trainer might want to catch a wild Pokémon to train them for future battles, evolve them, or trade them with other Trainers. Sometimes Pokémon and their Trainers just bond for life, like Ash and Pikachu!

Finding them is the easy part

Make sure you have the right tools available when you look for Pokémon. The right Poké Balls, fishing rods, and enticing snacks can all help when searching for Pokémon.

Gift and trade

Not all Pokémon need to be caught. Sometimes you just feel a connection with a wild Pokémon and they choose to join your team! Others can be gifted by a professor when you enter a new region or obtained through using a Pokémon trading machine.

CREATING A POKÉMON TEAM

A Pokémon Trainer can collect and train as many Pokémon as they like. Great Trainers will try to catch lots of Pokémon to learn about how to raise them. Trainers quickly discover which Pokémon like to work in a team and which prefer to work alone.

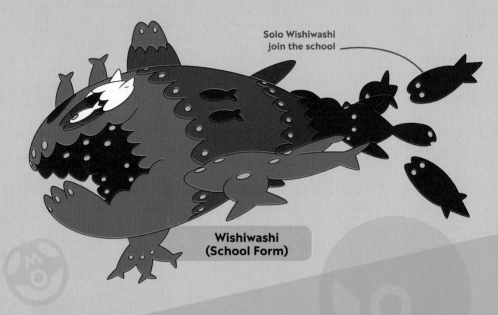

Solo Wishiwashi join the school

Wishiwashi
(School Form)

Great teams

Some Pokémon prefer to have lots of company. This gives them a sense of community or safety. A solo Wishiwashi is very weak, but when they team up, they can change into a powerful school form. While wild Dragonite might like to live in a large group on Dragonite Island.

Better solo

A few Pokémon like to work alone. For example, Prinplup can be a little snooty and think they are better than the rest of their team. They prefer a solitary life to teamwork.

Prinplup

Battle buddies

In battle, Pokémon Trainers can bring their best six Pokémon. Here are some top tips for choosing them:

- Pick the Pokémon you are most comfortable with.
- Try to match strengths against weaknesses.
- Remember to rest exhausted Pokémon!

Just my type

There are 18 known types of Pokémon, with new types still being discovered! The most important thing is to create a Pokémon team with types that work for you.

BIG AND SMALL

Pokémon come in all shapes and sizes, from the tiny Alcremie to tall Corviknight. When battling and catching new Pokémon, remember it is easier to pit Pokémon of the same size against each other. Battling a very large Pokémon using a smaller one can be tricky, but not impossible!

8 ft					
7 ft					
6 ft					
5 ft					
4 ft					
3 ft					
2 ft					
1 ft					
0 ft					

Ash	Pikachu	Alcremie	Corviknight	Drednaw
		1ft (0.3 m)	7ft 3in (2.2 m)	3ft 3in (1 m)

Does size matter?

Size isn't everything. An inexperienced Pokémon will have less stamina and skills than an experienced one. Also, Pokémon types are very important. For example, Water-type attacks have a stronger effect on Fire-type Pokémon. This could give a smaller Pokémon a chance to win!

Big heart

In the end, what matters most is the size of a Trainer and Pokémon's hearts. With courage, they can face any challenges!

2.5 m

2.0 m

1.5 m

1.0 m

0.5 m

0 m

Grookey
1ft (0.3 m)

Scorbunny
1ft (0.3 m)

Sobble
1ft (0.3 m)

Wooloo
2ft (0.6 m)

Yamper
1ft (0.3 m)

LIKE NIGHT AND DAY

When looking for a Pokémon, Trainers should remember that some prefer the dark of night, while others love a sunny day. Some have developed special skills, which help them thrive at their favorite time of day or night.

Noctowl

Night seekers

These Pokémon are most active during the night or in dark spaces. To adapt to the low light, Noivern hunts using special vibrations called ultrasonic waves, while Noctowl's eyes have developed to see clearly in the murkiest light!

Noivern

Strong wings for flying in the night

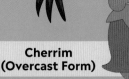

Cherrim
(Overcast Form)

Sunny creatures

On a bright day, it is possible to find these Pokémon outside enjoying the warmth! Grass-types like Cherrim and Skiploom often love sunlight.

Solrock

Flower blooms only if it is over 64°F (18°C)

Skiploom

Cherrim (Sunshine Form)

Use everything you have

Sometimes, you can wait day and night and still not find the Pokémon you are looking for. Try using lures, specialized Poké Balls, and snacks to bait shy Pokémon.

New Trainers should be wary of selecting Pokémon with dangerous physical features or aggressive personalities. These fierce Pokémon can be hard to catch, and even harder to train!

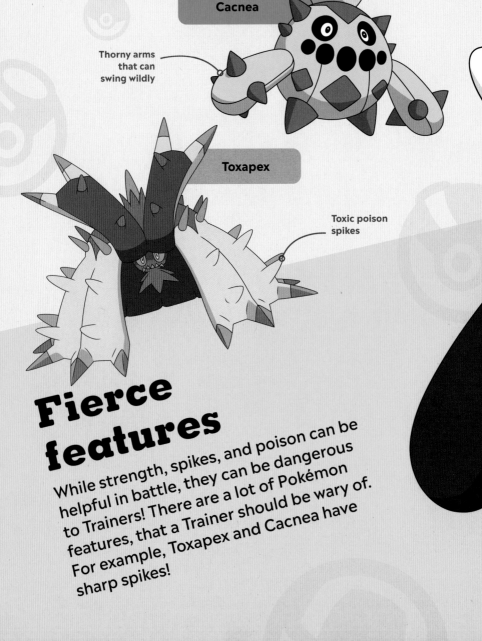

Cacnea

Thorny arms that can swing wildly

Toxapex

Toxic poison spikes

Fierce features

While strength, spikes, and poison can be helpful in battle, they can be dangerous to Trainers! There are a lot of Pokémon features, that a Trainer should be wary of. For example, Toxapex and Cacnea have sharp spikes!

Difficult creatures

A Pokémon's personality is sometimes scarier than their spikes! Liepard can be moody and vicious, while Drednaw is highly aggressive!

Liepard

Bewear

Dangerous Pokémon

These Pokémon also have qualities that can be a risk to their Trainers:

- Basculin can have a violent nature.
- Bewear are super strong and can accidentally crush their friends in a hug.
- Vileplume shake out clouds of toxic pollen with every step.

EVOLUTION

As your Pokémon grows in strength, it has the option to evolve! During Evolution, your Pokémon becomes more powerful and the name, size, and sometimes type might change.

A Raichu evolves from a Pikachu

A Pichu evolves into a Pikachu

How to evolve

Most Evolutions occur by training Pokémon and using them in battle. After a certain amount of experience, the Pokémon will evolve. There are also certain stones that can bring on an Evolution.

Eevee Normal

Eevee Water (Vaporeon)

Stages of Evolution

Most Pokémon Evolutions have three stages. For example, Pichu can evolve into Pikachu, then Raichu. However, some Pokémon, like Mew, don't evolve at all. Others like Munchlax evolve only once.

Why not evolve?

Why would you want Munchlax if Snorlax is more evolved? With first-stage Evolutions, Trainers can focus on different moves and skills. The Pokémon might also be happy the way it is and show no interest in evolving!

Munchlax

Unusual Evolutions

Eevee is the Evolution Pokémon. It is unique because it can evolve into eight different Pokémon! But once it evolves, it cannot evolve again.

Eevee Electric (Jolteon)

Eevee Fire (Flareon)

DIFFERENT FORMS

Evolution is not the only way Pokémon can change form. The appearance of some Pokémon can be affected by the environment they were raised in, the season, or even their gender.

Where are you from?

Sometimes a Pokémon's colors and features show where in the world they come from. You can see this in:

- Shellos, who can be pink or blue depending on if they grew up in the cold East Sea or warm West Sea.
- Pokémon like Burmy, who cover themselves in materials from their local surroundings.
- Variant Pokémon from each region who look a little different to the regular versions.

Plant-covered Burmy

Sand-covered Burmy

Trash-covered Burmy

Pokémon for all seasons

Sawsbuck change form throughout the year. Their fur can change color, and the plants in their horns will bloom depending on if it's winter, spring, summer, or fall.

Winter

Males and females

Sometimes you can tell what gender a Pokémon is by its appearance. For example, female Meowstic have mainly white fur, while males have mostly blue. These Pokémon might also have different personalities— female Meowstic are known for being a little more aggressive than males.

Meowstic
(Male Form)

Meowstic
(Female Form)

Spring

Summer

Fall

GETTING ALONG WITH YOUR POKÉMON

Now that you know how to catch, care for, and train your Pokémon, how can you tell if the two of you are compatible—or even friends? It is very important that you and your Pokémon are on the same page before going out into the world!

Communication is key

Pokémon don't usually speak, so it can be hard to know what they're thinking. But in a few cases, it is possible to understand what a Pokémon is telling you:

- Some Pokémon can communicate telepathically with their minds, like Mewtwo.
- Yamask can speak through people who wear it as a mask.
- Team Rocket's Meowth speaks human and often translates for other Pokémon.

Charizard

Frenemies

Many Pokémon and Trainers have disagreements! Ash had trouble when his Charmeleon evolved into a stubborn Charizard—and even Pikachu can be a handful! The best thing to do is keep learning about your Pokémon. The more you know their personality, the better you will get along.

Emolga

Let them rest

Pokémon Trainer Iris and her Emolga are a great team. Iris understands that Emolga likes to be cared for and rest in a Poké Ball. This helps them avoid fighting with each other!

CARING FOR YOUR POKÉMON

A HAPPY HOME

Many Pokémon will make their home in a Poké Ball. This protects them while training and traveling. But you can't just throw your Pokémon inside a Poké Ball without thought! Make sure their environment is safe and stress-free by:

- Picking a Poké Ball that is best for catching that type of Pokémon.
- Letting Pokémon battle in and visit their most comfortable areas (forests, seas, mountains, and caves).
- Keeping Pokémon healthy by taking them to a Pokémon Center often.

Combee

Combee love flowering fields

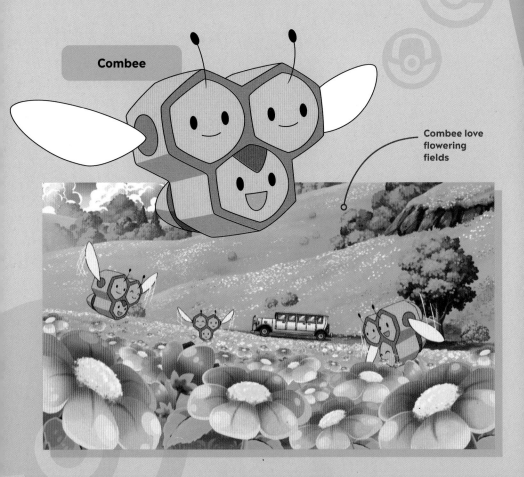

Aren't all Poké Balls the same?

A comfortable home is important for happy, healthy Pokémon. Some types of Poké Balls are better at catching and keeping Pokémon. For instance, Pokémon caught in a Luxury Ball bond with their Trainer more quickly.

Poké Ball interiors

The interior of a Poké Ball with a Pokémon inside it is a mystery. It has been rumored that Poké Balls read the data from the Pokémon inside and tailor their housing to keep that Pokémon safe and comfortable.

Free roamers

Not all Pokémon will agree to live in a Poké Ball. Ash's Pikachu prefers to stay in the open by Ash's side!

WHAT SHOULD YOU FEED A POKÉMON?

A good diet is key when it comes to training a Pokémon. Most Pokémon enjoy foods such as Poké Puffs and berries. Some Pokémon need special diets, and their Trainers create meals just for them!

Picky eater

Try these tips if your Pokémon is fussy about their food:

- Be patient.
- Try giving it new foods.
- Develop your own recipes to offer your Pokémon.

Tamato Berry

Sitrus Berry

Pecha Berry

Berry good

Berries form a large part of a Pokémon's diet. There are many types of berries with different flavors and even special qualities.

Oran Berry

Yummy treats

Many Pokémon have a sweet tooth and love sugary treats like macaroons and Poké Puffs. These tasty snacks can been found in the Kalos region.

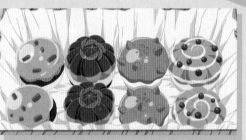

Natural nibbles

Pokémon also enjoy tasty food found in the wild. Teddiursa loves to lick sweet honey off its paws. The honey is made from pollen collected by Beedrill.

Hungry Pokémon

Some Pokémon need to eat more than others. Snorlax likes to eat 800 lb (360 kg) of food every day so will need a lot of feeding! Bulbasaur gets nutrition from the seed on its back so will need less food.

Snorlax

Belly full of food

NO PAIN, NO GAIN

Regular exercise is important for all living things to stay healthy. Some Pokémon enjoy physical activity more than others. In particular, Fighting-type Pokémon like to keep their bodies in tip-top shape!

Throh

Cruisin' for a bruisin'

All Pokémon exercise differently. Throh and Sawk use martial arts as their go-to exercises. While Pokémon like Machop and Machamp like to do strength-training workouts.

Sawk

Bounce it out

Exercise doesn't need to be all about fighting and battling! A Popplio might work out by bouncing balloons on its nose.

Popplio

Training for battle

Some Trainers put their Pokémon through tough training to prepare them for battles. They might make their Pokémon lift heavy weights to improve their strength. Others might develop special exercise tools to train their Pokémon.

Some Pokémon like to be pampered! Making your Pokémon feel comfortable is important— happy Pokémon are closer to their Trainer.

Furfrou

Hair today

Furfrou is known for being well groomed and styled by its Trainers. There are even contests to determine which is the best-looking Poodle Pokémon.

Fluffy, white fur

DIY

Some Pokémon, like Litten, are low-maintenance and groom themselves. That's a load off your hairbrush!

Litten

Feathers or scales?

Not all Pokémon can be groomed in the same way. Take Staravia and Magikarp. One has scales, while the other has feathers. Scaly Pokémon need a firm scrub brush, while feathered Pokémon like a much lighter, softer brush!

Soft feathers

Staravia

Magikarp

Tough scales

Spa break

A day at the spa makes everyone feel relaxed! Grooming and attending spas give Trainers and Pokémon a well -needed break.

Pokémon Paradise Springs Resort

FALLING IN SICK

There are a lot of reasons why a Pokémon might feel unwell. They may have an injury, be feeling weak after a battle, or just have a bad head cold! Some Pokémon will feel down if they see their Trainer is sad, too.

Checkup time!

When checking your Pokémon's health, remember to keep an eye on:

- Your Pokémon's color
- Your Pokémon's physical characteristics
- Your Pokémon's mood

Healthy signs

Some Pokémon have features that tell you if they are healthy. A Charmander's tail-flame should always be bright and intense. If it starts to go out, that might mean that your Charmander is sick!

Bright burning flame

Charmander

Snot and tail secretions

When Cubchoo's drippy snot dries up, it might be feeling unwell. Equally, a change in the color of Smeargle's tail secretion is also a sign that its mood may have worsened.

Happy green tail slime

Smeargle

Cubchoo

Healthy drippy snot

What you can't see

Keeping your Pokémon healthy with diet and exercise is only part of a Trainer's job. The better you get to know your Pokémon, the quicker you will be able to tell if something seems out of place.

HOW TO HEAL

What should you do if you notice that your Pokémon is sick? Luckily, there are a lot of medicines, remedies, and places you can go to heal your tired or hurt Pokémon.
Some options are:

- Take them to your nearest Pokémon Center.
- Heal them with herbal remedies, medicine, or berries.
- If you are in a battle, stop or switch out your Pokémon.

Be prepared

A good Trainer will always be prepared with healing berries and medicines while traveling with their Pokémon. Always try to stock up on healing salves and potions from the Poké Mart before long journeys or intense battles.

The Center of attention

When a Pokémon is injured or unwell, you should always try to find a Pokémon Center. They can be found in most towns and cities. The nurse in the Pokémon Center is named Nurse Joy. She and her Pokémon assistants will always do their best to bring a Pokémon back to health.

Hat with the Pokémon Center logo

Nurse's badge

Pocket for nurse supplies

Fluffy ears to listen to patients

Reassuring expression

Wigglytuff

Don't battle

An easy way to avoid injury is to be prepared to pull your Pokémon from battles and not use them again until they are fully healed.

HOW TO BATTLE POKÉMON EFFECTIVELY

Battling is a large part of a Pokémon's life and all Pokémon approach it differently. Battles can develop a Pokémon's confidence and skills. A good team will have Pokémon who enjoy battling and work well with others.

Primarina

Why battle?

Some Pokémon fight because they love the thrill of competition, while others are amazingly skilled at it. For Primarina, every battle is a stage, and this Pokémon loves to show off its dramatic battle moves.

Master of all types

It is a good idea to teach your Pokémon different types of moves. This will give them a strong chance against all types of attacks!

Type cast

It is important to learn which types of Pokémon are strong or weak against other types. Pokémon trained in Fire-type moves, like Chimchar, might be weak against Water-type Pokémon. You can find all this information in your Pokédex!

Lead well

Pokémon and their Trainers are a close team. If you lack confidence and feel unsure, your Pokémon will, too! To turn you and your Pokémon into a battle-winning team, you'll need:

- A Pokémon's trust
- A comfortable, well-rested Pokémon
- Knowledge of Pokémon types and moves
- Confidence in your Pokémon training

Editor Nicole Reynolds
Designers James McKeag and Thelma-Jane Robb
Senior Production Editor Marc Staples
Senior Production Controller Lloyd Robertson
Managing Editor Paula Regan
Managing Art Editor Jo Connor
Publishing Director Mark Searle

DK would like to thank Hank Woon and the rest of the team at
The Pokémon Company International. Also, at DK, Ruth Amos and Lisa Stock
for editorial assistance and Jennette ElNaggar for proofreading.

Author dedication: To my children, Emily and Nicholas, who are far greater
Pokémon experts than me, and who helped to write this book.

First American Edition, 2021
Published in the United States by DK Publishing
1450 Broadway, Suite 801, New York, NY 10018

Page design copyright © 2021 Dorling Kindersley Limited
DK, a Division of Penguin Random House LLC
21 22 23 24 25 10 9 8 7 6 5 4 3 2 1
001–325210–Oct/2021

©2021 Pokémon. © 1997-2020 Nintendo, Creatures, GAME FREAK,
TV Tokyo, ShoPro, JR Kikaku. TM, ®Nintendo.

A catalog record for this book
is available from the Library of Congress.
ISBN 978-0-7440-4278-8

DK books are available at special discounts when
purchased in bulk for sales promotions, premiums,
fund-raising, or educational use. For details, contact:
DK Publishing Special Markets, 1450 Broadway,
Suite 801, New York, NY 10018. SpecialSales@dk.com

Printed and bound in China

For the curious
www.dk.com

This book was made with Forest Stewardship
Council ™ certified paper—one small step in
DK's commitment to a sustainable future.
For more information go to
www.dk.com/our-green-pledge